How to Draw Cool Ships and Boats

from Sailboats to Ocean Liners

BARRON'S

Created and produced by Green Android Ltd
Illustrated by Fiona Gowen

First edition for North America published in 2018
by Barron's Educational Series, Inc.

All inquiries should be addressed to:
Barron's Educational Series, Inc.
250 Wireless Boulevard
Hauppauge, NY 11788
www.barronseduc.com

ISBN: 978-1-4380-1056-4

Library of Congress Control No.: 2017948411

Date of Manufacture: October 2017
Manufactured by: Toppan Leefung Printing Co., Ltd., Shenzhen, China

Printed in China
9 8 7 6 5 4 3 2 1

Contents

Page 32 has an index of everything to draw in this book.

How to Draw
Canadian Canoe

Canoes, which date from 8040 B.C.E., are pointed at both ends. A sitting or kneeling canoeist uses a single-bladed paddle. Traditionally made of wood, modern craft are made from fiberglass or aluminum.

Dragon Boat

Pedal Boat

1 Starting at the bow (front), draw the keel to the stern. Then, draw the rest of the hull.

Thor Heyerdahl's Kon-Tiki

2 Draw the gunwale—the top edge along the sides of the canoe.

3 Pencil in the canoeist and the single-bladed paddle.

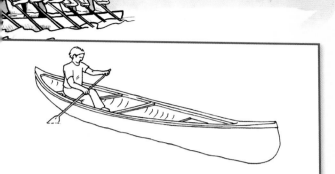

4 Draw the canoeist's stern bench, the bow bench, and thwart (the crossbar that braces the sides of the canoe).

5 Sketch in the ruffled water surface, especially around where the paddle strikes the water.

Canadian Canoe

6 To finish, strengthen the outlines, and add light shading to the keel and the canoe's interior.

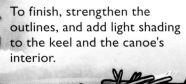

Outrigger Canoe

Venetian Gondola

Row Boat

Dugout Canoe

Inflatable Dinghy

Wooden Raft

Coracle

Punt

Kayak

Aymara Reed Boat

Viking Longship

At 98 feet (30 m) long, this replica of a 975-year-old Viking warship had 60 oarsmen to speed it across open seas. It is double-ended, which means it can change direction without having to turn around.

1 Draw the rippled waterline. Then, draw the shapely stern and bow. Add the rudder oar.

2 Sketch the mainsail, adding detail to the yard (the rod that holds the sail's uppermost rigging).

3 Lightly pencil in the gunwale—the top edge of the boat's side. Draw 14 shields.

4 Draw the head of a rower behind each shield, and draw the oars. Pencil in the top of the mast.

5 Sketch in the rudder oarsman, the pattern on the mainsail, and the rigging ropes.

Viking
Longship

6 To finish, strengthen the outlines, and add shading and texture to the water, hull, and mainsail.

Viking
Cargo Boat

All-weather Lifeboat

This 23-foot- (7-m-) long lifeboat can cope with severe conditions. Should it capsize, it is self-righting. It has a crew of seven, an inflatable dinghy that is hoisted off, and medical equipment.

1 Draw the waterline. Then, draw the bow, stern, and deck. Add gunwale and stern details.

2 Pencil in the outline of the wheelhouse, main cabin, and flying bridge.

3 Add details like bow bollard, windows, dinghy (on wheelhouse roof), and guardrail.

Tugboat

Shrimp Fishing Boats

Inshore Lifeboat

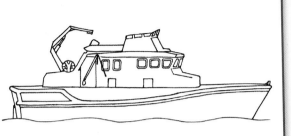

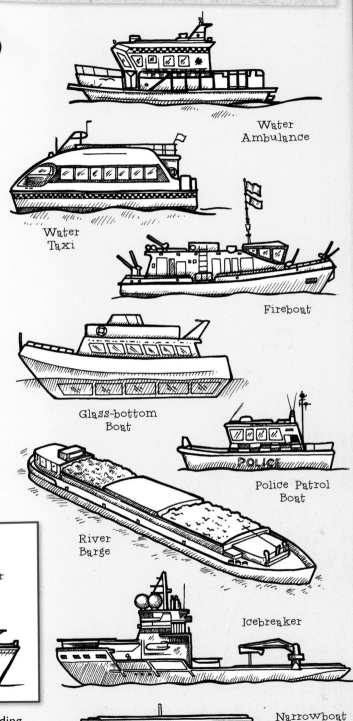

Water
Ambulance

Water
Taxi

Fireboat

Glass-bottom
Boat

Police Patrol
Boat

River
Barge

Icebreaker

Narrowboat

4 Draw the dinghy-lifting crane and lifebuoy. Add more detail to the wheelhouse.

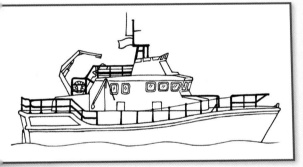

5 Add more guardrails, and draw the antenna and radar on the flying bridge.

All-weather
Lifeboat

6 Finish by strengthening the outlines. Add shading to the vessel (especially along the waterline) and dinghy, and texture to the water.

Brigantine Pirate Ship

Because they were fast and agile, many 17th-century pirates used brigantine vessels. The bow's high deck made it easy to board other ships. The skull and crossbones meant no mercy would be shown.

1 Draw the ruffled waterline, pointed bow, raised quarterdeck, and rudder.

2 Pencil in the guardrails, anchor, gunports, and hull belays to which rigging is attached.

3 Draw the mast, mainsails, and crow's nest. Erase any unwanted lines.

Brigantine
Pirate Ship

4 Draw two more masts and their sails. On the bow, draw a bowsprit and sail.

5 Sketch the rigging, ratlines (rope netting behind the main mast), and flag. Add detail to the sails and texture to the water.

6 Finish by adding shading to the hull above the waterline and to the lower edges of the sails. Strengthen the outlines.

11

How to Draw
U.S. Brig Niagara

This 1813 wooden sailing ship is a 108-foot (33-m) brig vessel. Brigs were used as warships, carrying 10 to 18 guns, and for cargo. The famous brig ship, *Niagara*, is now a training vessel for the U.S. Coast Guard.

1 Draw the waterline, stern, bow, and gunwale. Then, add the long bowsprit.

2 Sketch three sails on the bowsprit (railing along the deck), and draw portholes.

3 Pencil in the mast, and align it with the bowsprit sails, as show Pencil in the bottom yardarm c the mast, sails, and low cabin.

4 Draw the second mast, sails, yardarm, and flag. Then, add the gaff sail between the masts.

USS *Niagara*'s Commodore Perry

12

In the Age of Sail (1571–1862) trade, exploration, and naval warfare were ruled by different types of sailing ships.

5 Draw a second gaff sail off the rear mast, and a flag. Sketch in ratlines (rope netting).

U.S. Brig Niagara

6 To finish, strengthen the outlines, and add shading to the sails, flags, and hull. Shade in segments of the cabin.

Cutter

Carrack

Clipper

Caravel

Galleon

Man O' War

Cog

Sloop

Cargo Brig

Schooner

Powered by the Wind

Craft that set sails to catch the wind are called sailboats or yachts. They are used for recreation, sport (including extraordinary around-the-world challenges), and racing. They range in size from 13 to 460 feet (4 to 140 m).

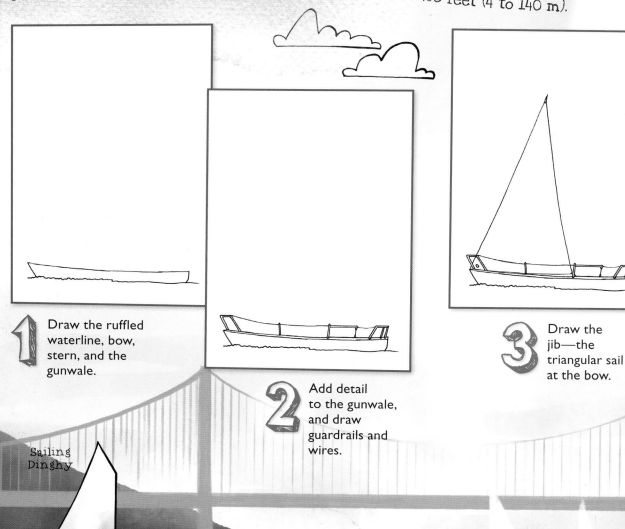

1 Draw the ruffled waterline, bow, stern, and the gunwale.

2 Add detail to the gunwale, and draw guardrails and wires.

3 Draw the jib—the triangular sail at the bow.

Sailing Dinghy

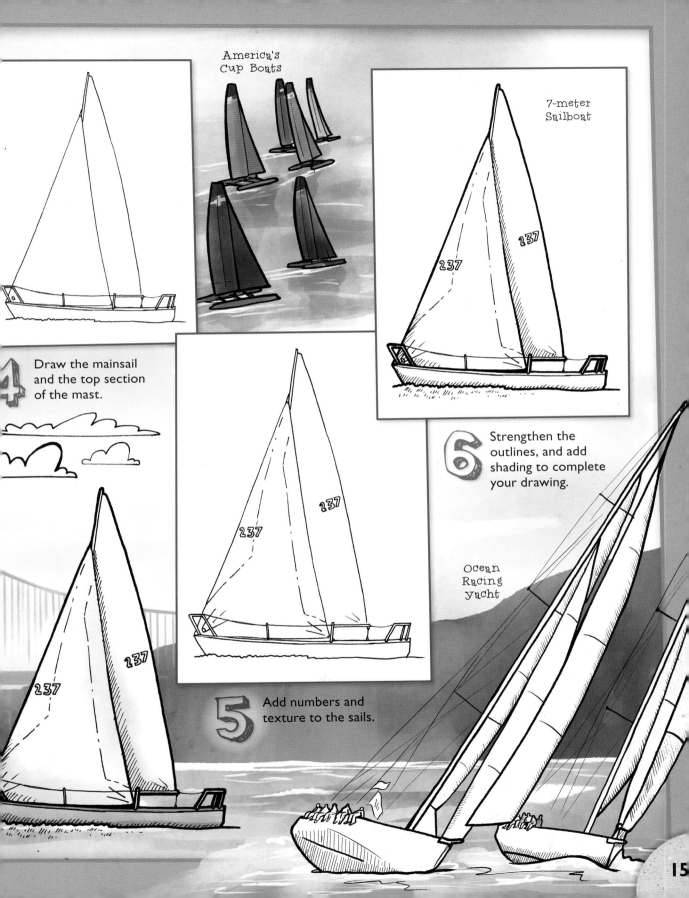

America's
Cup Boats

7-meter
Sailboat

237 237

Draw the mainsail
and the top section
of the mast.

237 237

Strengthen the
outlines, and add
shading to complete
your drawing.

Ocean
Racing
Yacht

237 237

Add numbers and
texture to the sails.

237

How to Draw

Powerboats

Also called motorboats and speedboats, powerboats are powered by an engine mounted on the stern (outboard) or fitted in the hull (inboard). They are used for transportation, recreation, fishing, racing, and as working craft.

1 Draw the waterline. Then, draw the bow, stern, and gunwale.

2 Pencil in the cockpit, cabin, and flying bridge.

3 Add the stablizing fin to the flying bridge. This fin keeps the stern down when the boat travels at high speeds.

Wooden Motor Yacht

Rigid Inflatable Boat

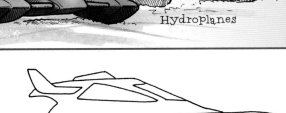
Hydroplanes

More to Draw

There are thousands of powerboat types—some for river cruising, others for breakneck speeds offshore.

Cabin Cruiser

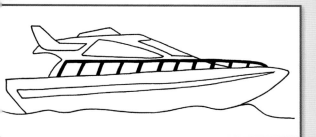

Draw the cockpit windows and detail on the hull.

Open Launch

Jet Ski

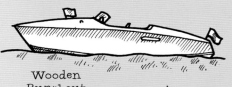
Wooden Runabout

Draw the guardrail and uprights using heavy thick lines.

Sport Yacht

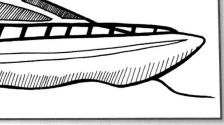
Speedboat

Offshore Go-fast Boat

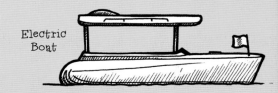
Electric Boat

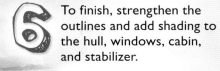

To finish, strengthen the outlines and add shading to the hull, windows, cabin, and stabilizer.

Speedboat and Skier

How to Draw
Fishing Trawler

This commercial boat is a dragger because its nets are dragged through the water. The trawls are cast and hauled in by mechanized hoists and winches. Large factory trawlers can process their catch.

1 Draw the waterline, bow, stern, and gunwale.

2 Draw the pilot house and windows. Add rear deck structures, including gantry.

3 Draw the tire fenders on the hull and rear deck. Add de to the gantry

Factory Trawler

Fishing Boat

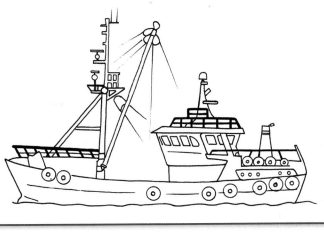

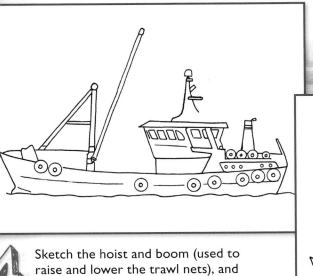

4 Sketch the hoist and boom (used to raise and lower the trawl nets), and radar mast on the pilot house.

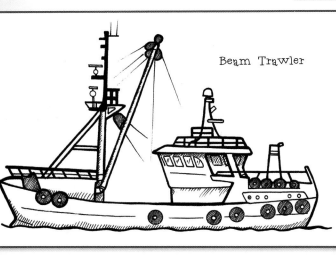

Beam Trawler

5 Add the guardrails, block and tackle on the boom arm, and antenna on the hoist.

6 Strengthen the outlines. Finish by adding texture to the water and shading to the trawler.

Outrigger Trawler

How to Draw
RMS Titanic

Designed to be "unsinkable" when launched in 1911, this passenger liner sank after hitting an iceberg on its maiden voyage. Around 1,500 people died in the icy waters of the North Atlantic Ocean.

Christo
Colun

1 Draw the waterline, bow, stern, and sleek hull.

2 Sketch in the deck-level ar first floor structure, and a details to the bow and ste

3 Draw another layer of deck structure.

Clipper Ship *Cutty Sark*

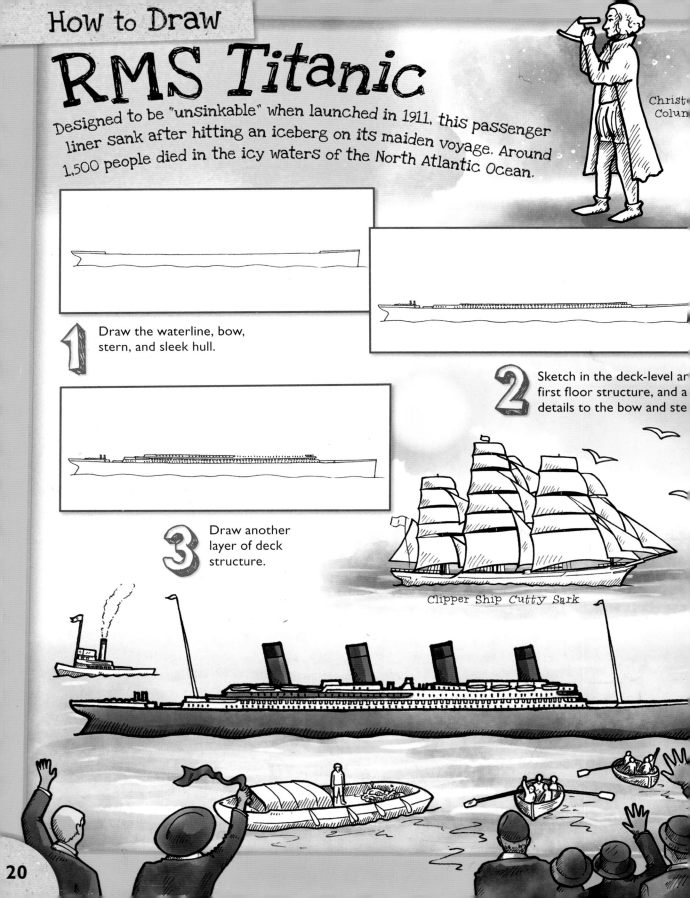

More to Draw

These famous ships carried sailors into battle, explorers to new lands, and innovated naval design.

Captain Scott's *Terra Nova*

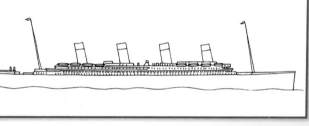

4 Draw the top decks, including life rafts, and slanting masts at the bow and stern.

Charles Darwin's *HMS Beagle*

Lord Nelson's *HMS Victory*

5 Draw the four backward slanting funnels on the top of the deck structure.

Captain Cook's *HMS Endeavour*

Columbus's *Santa Maria*

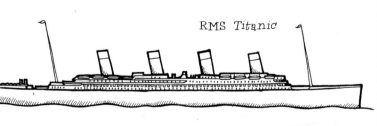

RMS *Titanic*

USS *Constitution*

6 Strengthen the outlines, and add shading to complete the RMS *Titanic*.

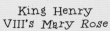

HMS *Dreadnought*

King Henry VIII's *Mary Rose*

Vessels of the Deep

The first submarine (1775) had a hand-turned propeller and air for 30 minutes. The U-boats and submarines of the 1940s had diesel-electric motors, but today's nuclear subs can stay submerged for 25 years!

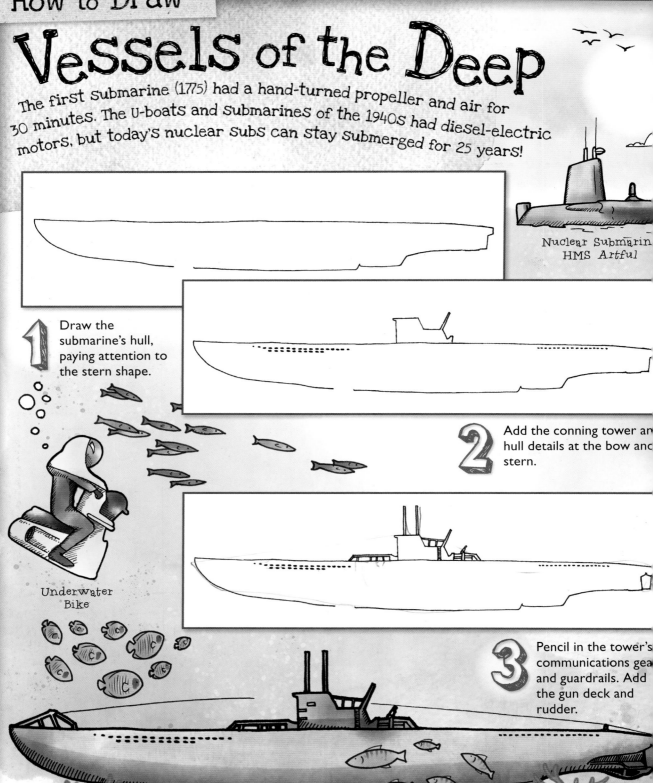

Nuclear Submarine
HMS *Artful*

1 Draw the submarine's hull, paying attention to the stern shape.

Underwater Bike

2 Add the conning tower and hull details at the bow and stern.

3 Pencil in the tower's communications gear and guardrails. Add the gun deck and rudder.

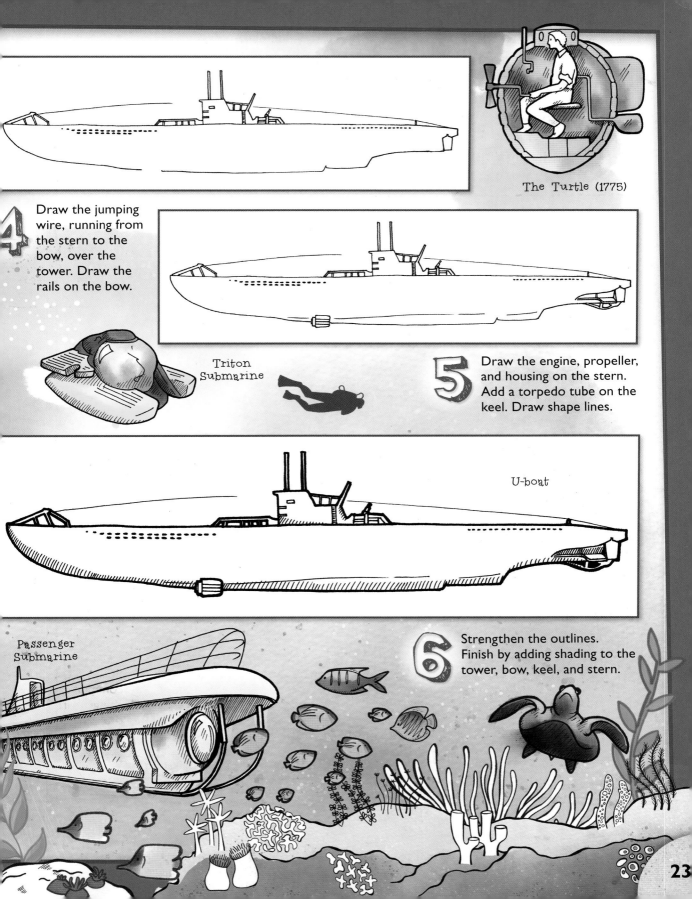

The Turtle (1775)

4 Draw the jumping wire, running from the stern to the bow, over the tower. Draw the rails on the bow.

Triton Submarine

5 Draw the engine, propeller, and housing on the stern. Add a torpedo tube on the keel. Draw shape lines.

U-boat

Passenger Submarine

6 Strengthen the outlines. Finish by adding shading to the tower, bow, keel, and stern.

Giants on the High Seas

The largest ships plying the oceans are the container ships—a few are the size of four football fields. The super-vessels can load 16,000 containers (some can load 30,000 containers), and have a top speed of 29 mph (46 kph).

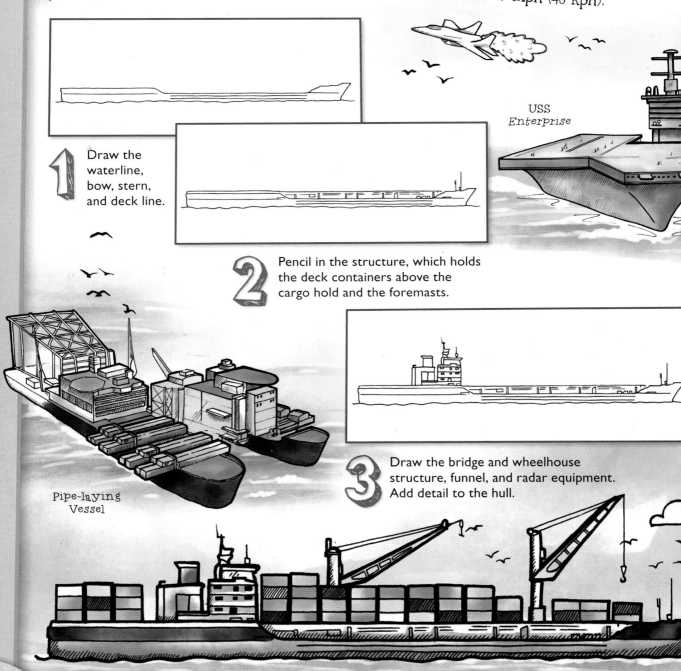

1 Draw the waterline, bow, stern, and deck line.

USS Enterprise

2 Pencil in the structure, which holds the deck containers above the cargo hold and the foremasts.

Pipe-laying Vessel

3 Draw the bridge and wheelhouse structure, funnel, and radar equipment. Add detail to the hull.

More to Draw

Giant ships measure up to 1,312 feet (400 m), and can carry 6,700 passengers, two million barrels of oil, or 60 planes.

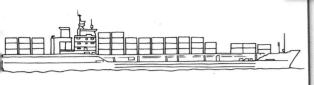

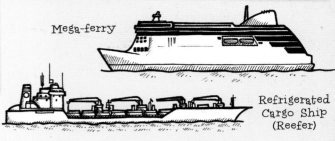

Mega-ferry

Refrigerated Cargo Ship (Reefer)

4 Draw neat towers of containers along the deck.

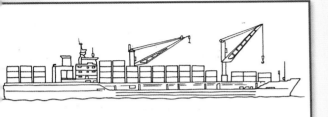

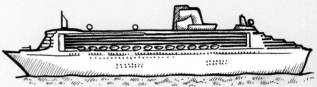

RMS Queen Mary 2 Ocean Liner

5 Sketch the pair of cargo cranes, adding detail as you draw.

Passenger Ferry

Container Ship

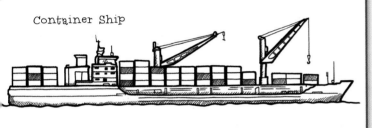

Bulk Carrier

Warship

6 Strengthen the outlines, and add shading to the container ship to complete your drawing.

Liquid Natural Gas Carrier

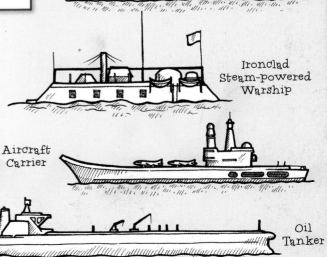

Ironclad Steam-powered Warship

Aircraft Carrier

Oil Tanker

Paddle Steamer

In original riverboats, steam powered the paddle wheels, which could be 56 feet (17 m) in diameter, but later boats had diesel engines. Designed for carrying cargo and passengers on rivers, lakes, or inshore waters, some are oceangoing.

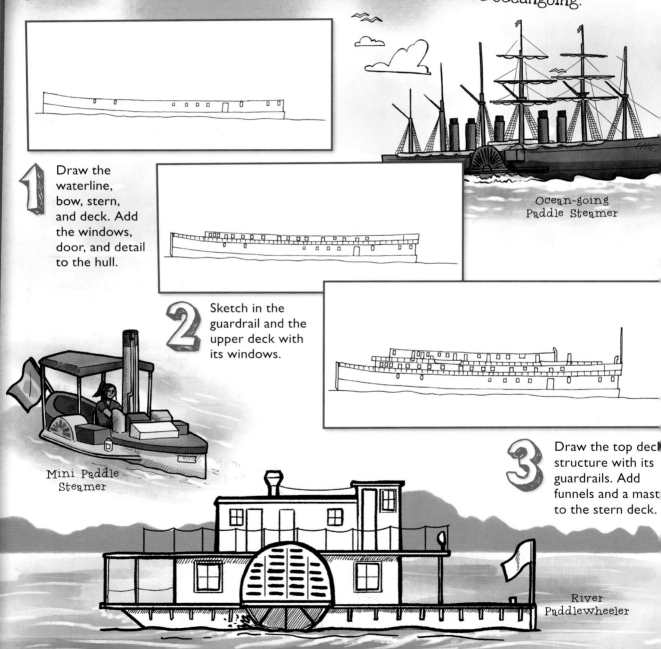

1 Draw the waterline, bow, stern, and deck. Add the windows, door, and detail to the hull.

Ocean-going Paddle Steamer

2 Sketch in the guardrail and the upper deck with its windows.

Mini Paddle Steamer

3 Draw the top deck structure with its guardrails. Add funnels and a mast to the stern deck.

River Paddlewheeler

Clyde Steamer

4 Pencil in the wheelhouse and its windows, and all the masts and funnels.

Clermont
Paddle Steamer

5 Draw the wires and cables. Then, draw the paddlewheel, its housing, and water spray on the stern.

Creole Queen Paddlewheeler

Human-powered
Paddle Wheel

6 Finish by strengthening the outlines. Add shading to the hull above the waterline, and add texture to the water surface.

How to Draw

Hydrofoils

Hydrofoil Kaya

As the vessel gains speed, the foils (winged-shaped feet) attached to struts lift the hull out of the water, reducing drag and increasing speed. Hydrofoil technology is mostly used for rapid commuter services and some sports vessels.

1 Draw the waterline and waves. Add the bow and stern struts and the boat's hull.

Hydrofoil Trimaran

2 Carefully pencil in the outline of the boat's double-decked structure.

3 Draw the three long horizontal lines. Then, fill in other details, including the radar.

Foiling
Dinghy

Draw the windows, a door,
guardrails, and equipment on
the wheelhouse.

Human-powered
Hydrofoil Vessel

Pencil in the life raft
containers on the upper
deck, the three masts,
and the aerials.

Jetfoil
Hydrofoil

Strengthen the outlines, and
add shading to complete your
drawing of the hydrofoil.

Ancient Boats

Humans have used watercraft for exploration, trade, and fishing for millennia. An early sea route crossed the Arabian Sea, so navigation skills were known. The 1,800-year-old Chinese junk is still used today!

Ancient Polynesian Voyaging Canoe

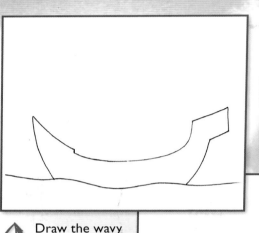

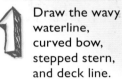
1 Draw the wavy waterline, curved bow, stepped stern, and deck line.

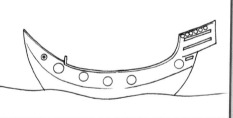

2 Pencil in a "painted eye" on the bow, decorative disks to the hull, and stern deck detail.

3 Draw the bowsprit with its penna and sail. Then, draw rails along th deck and flags to the stern.

4 Draw two bamboo-battened sails and one normal sail. Then, draw the masts.

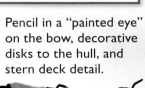

Peruvian Reed Boat

Below are different types of boats designed by ancient cultures from the four corners of the world.

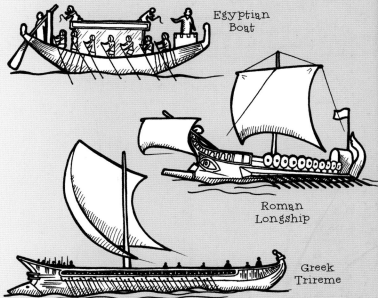

Egyptian Boat

Roman Longship

Greek Trireme

Sketch the sails and pennants on top of each mast, and add a genoa sail on the bow.

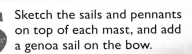

Early Native American Canoe

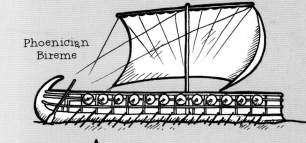

Phoenician Bireme

Chinese Junk

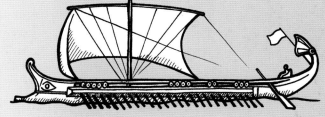

Greek Galley (Penteconter)

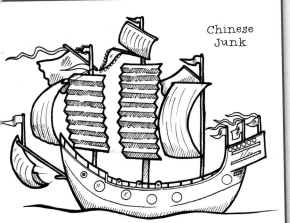

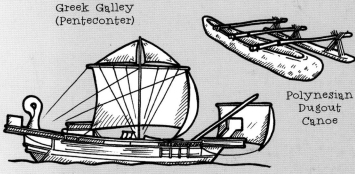

Polynesian Dugout Canoe

Strengthen the outlines. Add shading to the bamboo-batten sails to complete your Chinese junk.

Roman Cargo Boat

Index

This index is in alphabetical order, and it lists all the watercraft—over 100—that are in this book so that you can easily find your favorites.